GOD STILL LOVES ME

7- DAILY AFFIRMATIONS & PRAYERS FOR KIDS

Written By

Denisecia Lee

Illustrations by

Samon Roy

Gemlight Publishing LLC
Southlake, Texas

© Copyright by Denisecia Lee
God Still Loves Me.

All rights reserved.No part of this publication may be reproduced, in any form, or by any means,
electronic or mechanical, including photocopying, recording, or any other means without the prior written permission of the publisher, with the exception of brief quotations embodied in critical reviews and other non-commercial uses permitted by copyright law. For permission, requests correspond to the publisher at the address below. Address correspondence as "Attention: "Gemlight Administrator."
Scripture quotations are taken from the King James Bible.

Illustrations by: Samon Roy
ISBN: 978-1-7367934-8-0

Gemlight Publishing LLC
2600 E. Southlake Blvd. STE 120-377
Southlake, Texas 76092
gemlightpublishing.com

Ordering Information: Special discounts are available on quantity purchases by corporations, associations, and other groups. For details, contact the publisher at the address above. For orders by U.S.A. trade bookstores and wholesalers, please contact Gemlight Distribution:
Tel: (833) 436-5483)
or visit gemlightpublishing.com.
Printed in the United States of America.

DEDICATION

To my beautiful daughters, Grace and Legacy. As you journey and discover who you are, I pray that you are constantly reminded that God loves you. Thank you for being my daily inspiration and the reason why I wrote this book. There is no end to my love for both of you!

To my nieces, nephews, godchildren, former students, and any children I have had the privilege to be connected with, know that you are loved and worthy of everything God has for you.

NO ONE IS PERFECT!

Going to school is not always easy and enjoyable, especially when we are not in a good mood. On the way to school, I made a bad mistake yelling at my brother. He sat in my favorite seat in the car. "Get out of my seat," I yelled.

Maybe I should say sorry, I thought.

God still loves me!

THIS IS HOW GOD LOVES ME
James 3:2

For in many things we offend all. If any man offend not in word, the same is a perfect man, and able also to bridle the whole body.

I WILL GET THROUGH THIS

Today, at recess several kids didn't want to play with me. It made me very sad. I was about to walk away from the playground, when someone ran up to me. "Hey, do you want to play tag?"

God still loves me!

THIS IS HOW GOD LOVES ME
Psalm 144:15

Happy is that people, that is in such a case: yea, happy is that people, whose God is the LORD.

I ACCEPT ME

Some days I don't feel pretty. I don't like my hair and my legs are so skinny.

God still loves me!

THIS IS HOW GOD LOVES ME
Song of Solomon 4:7

Thou art all fair, my love; there is no spot in thee.

I AM SPECIAL

My friend betrayed me. My classmates laughed and pointed at me. Today my friends called me weird and strange. I was angry.

I was reminded that we are set-part. I am called to be different.

God still loves me!

THIS IS HOW GOD LOVES ME
1 Peter 2:9

But ye are a chosen generation, a royal priesthood, an holy nation, a peculiar people; that ye should shew forth the praises of him who hath called you out of darkness into his marvellous light.

I WILL ACCEPT CHRIST

I worked up the courage to ask Mom for a bike. She didn't give me a bike. Instead, she gave me a Bible.

"Ugh!" I shouted.

That night I tossed, turned, and tumbled out of bed.

"Why did you give me a Bible God? I wanted a bike. I thought you loved me."

My hands peeled back the first few pages of my Bible, and what did I learn?

God still loves me!

THIS IS HOW GOD LOVES ME
John 3:16

For God so loved the world, that he gave his only begotten Son, that whoever believeth in him should not perish, but have everlasting life.

I AM PROTECTED

Getting ready for bed that night I looked in the mirror, and what did I see?

The precious gift of life looking back at me. Thank you for protecting my family and I today.

God still and will always love me.

THIS IS HOW GOD LOVES ME
Psalm 36:7

How excellent is thy loving kindness O God! therefore the children of men put their trust under the shadow of thy wings.

7 Daily Affirmations & Prayers

7 Daily Affirmations & Prayers

Day 1:

I am part of God's will. I am not a mistake. God was intentional when He made me! Grace covers each step that I take today. Before I walk out the door today, I choose to kneel and pray.

Prayer

Lord, help me to be all that you created me to be. Watch over my family and I as we do your will. I know you have a plan for me. Amen!

My Thoughts

_____
_____
_____
_____
_____
_____
_____
_____
_____
_____
_____
_____
_____
_____

7 Daily Affirmations & Prayers

Day 2:

I am not forgotten or abandoned. I choose to fully accept Christ. I am always on God's mind. I was created in His image and likeness. I will not fear. God knows my steps.

Prayer

Lord, help me to love the way that you love. Please help me love all of me, no matter what others think about me. I am who God created me to be. Amen!

My Thoughts

_____
_____
_____
_____
_____
_____
_____
_____
_____
_____
_____
_____
_____
_____
_____

7 Daily Affirmations & Prayers

Day 3:

I am God's work. I miss and lack nothing. Everything I need is in him. When I am weak, I find my strength in Him. I will rest in His faithfulness.

Prayer

Lord, you are so faithful. Thank you for being kind and present in my life. What you have already provided for me is more than enough. Help me to be grateful and aware of what you have destined for me. Amen!

My Thoughts

_____
_____
_____
_____
_____
_____
_____
_____
_____
_____
_____
_____
_____
_____

7 Daily Affirmations & Prayers

Day 4:

I am loved. Even when I don't feel loved I know that I am. I have people who love and respect me.

Prayer

Lord, help me to love others the way that you love them. Help me to forgive even those that offend me. I thank you for not letting me be controlled by my emotions. Help me to discover the gifts and talents that you created in me so that I may bring you glory. In the name of Jesus, Amen!

My Thoughts

_____
_____
_____
_____
_____
_____
_____
_____
_____
_____
_____
_____
_____
_____

7 Daily Affirmations & Prayers

Day 5

I am strong. I am smart. I am wonderful. I am courageous. I am full of purpose, I am enough!

Prayer

Lord, help me to authentically be who you created me to be every day. Your guidance and gifts help me be fully present as I strive to make my dreams come true. I trust you. Amen!

My Thoughts

_____
_____
_____
_____
_____
_____
_____
_____
_____
_____
_____
_____
_____
_____

7 Daily Affirmations & Prayers

Day 6:

I fully embrace the will of my Father. I will walk with my head high because I know who I am.

Prayer

Lord, help me be a light to my friends and family so they see that you are real. Remind me of your power and might when I am afraid. Defeat my enemies and put my doubts away. In the name of Jesus.

My Thoughts

_____
_____
_____
_____
_____
_____
_____
_____
_____
_____
_____
_____
_____
_____
_____

7 Daily Affirmations & Prayers

Day 7:

I am transforming and evolving into whom Christ has created me to be. I will not fear the unknown. My life is in Jesus Christ. I will enjoy this journey. I am ready to step into the glory of God.

Prayer

Lord, thank you for your forgiveness. Help me forgive myself for past mistakes and to be confident each day. Lord, have your way. Where you lead me, I will follow.

My Thoughts

_____
_____
_____
_____
_____
_____
_____
_____
_____
_____
_____
_____
_____
_____

ABOUT THE AUTHOR

Denisecia Lee is a children's novelist who began writing in the later part of elementary school. Writing was a way to escape the economically disadvantaged neighborhood and the violence surrounding her. It was her safe place. She began writing her feelings and thoughts, and soon after that, she began to write her fears, worries, and concerns in diary entries. As she grew up and left for college at the University of Texas at Arlington, she began writing poetry, news stories, and short stories. Her work has been published by the UT Arlington Shorthorn and the Tarrant County College Collegian, the student news publication.

Denisecia resides in Arlington, Texas, with her husband and two beautiful daughters. Currently, she is an English teacher at Young Men's Leadership Academy in Fort Worth. She is also the newest North Texas Regional Board member for Reading Partners, where she serves as an advocate and voice for her local community.

www.ingramcontent.com/pod-product-compliance
Lightning Source LLC
Chambersburg PA
CBHW050806220426
43209CB00088BA/1649